BUSINESS COMMUNICATION: A HANDBOOK FOR SUCCESSFUL COMMUNICATION IN AN ORGANIZATION

MADISON E. BONHAM

Table of Content

DEVELOPING GOOD COMMUNICATION SKILLS AS AN ORGANIZATION

CHAPTER 4

USING EFFECTIVE COMMUNICATION TO BUILD STABLE WORK RELATIONSHIP

Why is good communication in the workplace crucial?

Types of Communication in a Workplace

How to Improve the Effectiveness of Workplace Communications

INTRODUCTION

Regardless of an organization's size, location, or objective, effective business communication skills are essential to its success. The internal culture and outward image of every corporation are intertwined with business communication. The organization's ability to educate, persuade, foster positive relationships, and improve communication inside the organization will thus depend on this. Effective business communication procedures help to build goodwill inside the company. Organizations must adapt to the continually changing environment in order to survive.

The communication procedures are organized and supplied in response to global problems. Internal communication is shown by the current conferencing, meetings, etc. while individuals are communicating.

These individuals might be clients, consumers,

distributors, dealers, media,

Business is impacted by all of this communication.

When done carefully, this kind of communication may

support the goal of influencing behavior to bring about

change. The fundamental issue in any company is

continuing to have excellent written and face-to-face

communication. The meaning that is truly understood

may not be what the other business interests are when it

comes to memos, reports, office orders, circulars, faxes,

and video communication. Otherwise, it will give the

company a bad reputation and can hurt the messages that

are sent between them. When individuals inside the

organization speak, they are sending the appropriate

message. Realize that there are two distinct cultural,

technological, and competitive backgrounds for the speaker and the listener. Generally speaking, all businesses want to succeed. It could be legitimate or not. Workers, owners and employees, buyers and sellers, service providers and consumers are just a few examples of internal communication channels. The effectiveness of internal communication greatly affects how much business is done. It occurs between different groups of communication process, inside companies, in markets and market venues, and between different corporate entities. Communication issues are often caused by management issues.

Orders are not comprehended correctly, which results in serious blunders. the main issue with consumers and potential customers as well as with internal company employees and press representatives.

a business's interest. Any organization relies on communication to function, but because every organization's key players have their own limitations and a variety of things can occur to alter the workforce's dynamic nature, internal communication can be difficult to execute when done against other key players. They do this to cooperate as a team and realize that when an organization communicates with someone outside the organization, this is known as external communication. Examples of external communication include government, the general public, and others.

Madison.

CHAPTER 1

BUSINESS

COMMUNICATION

Definition of Business

Communication.

Modern firms must have effective business communication because it helps them achieve their objectives, forge connections, and promote cooperation and collaboration. Success in today's fast-paced and cutthroat corporate world depends on effective business communication. It makes it possible for businesses to accomplish their objectives, create connections, and promote cooperation and teamwork. For professional development and career progress, strong business communication skills are also necessary. Building respect and trust, promoting collaboration, and increasing overall productivity can all be facilitated by sending messages that are clear and concise and in line with the company's goals and objectives. On the other hand, insufficient communication can result in errors, disagreements, and low morale. Various academics have provided various definitions of business communication. Several of them are listed below:

Business communication is a system that is in charge of bringing about change across the board, according to **Ricks and Gow.**

Business communication, according to **W.H.**, is the sharing of various viewpoints, ideas, and news among related parties.

According to **Prof. J. Haste,** business communication refers to any exchange of information between two or more businesspeople for the purpose of efficiently organizing and managing a business.

In order to accomplish organizational goals, management and employees must communicate effectively. Reducing errors is intended to increase organizational efficiency. Marketing, public relations, customer service, corporate and interpersonal communication are just a few examples of the various aspects of business communication.

Components of Business

Communication

- Sender: The sender is the one who created the message and is in charge of communicating the contents to the receiver.

- Business information:This is the information that the sender wants the recipient to know. The message can be delivered using written or spoken words, pictures, or nonverbal cues.

- Receiver: The receiver who gets a communication from a sender is the recipient. The message must be understandable by the recipient in order for them to respond to the sender.

- Feedback: Feedback is the declaration made to the sender by the recipient that the message has been appropriately comprehended. In order to guarantee that the message has been delivered precisely and successfully, feedback is a crucial component of the communication process.

The aforementioned components point to business communication as a process where information or news relating to business is transmitted between various business partners for the goal of efficient business administration, such as customers, suppliers, business clients, workers, etc.

Additionally, it requires a consistent flow of information, and feedback is seen as a vital and significant component of corporate communication. Because there are many individuals involved and there are several levels of hierarchy, business communication is crucial for planning, coordinating, organizing, directing, and regulating among other management activities.

SCOPE OF BUSINESS COMMUNICATION IN AN ORGANIZATION

A broad variety of tasks that are crucial to the operation of contemporary businesses are included in the scope of business communication. Among the crucial components of corporate communication are:

Internal Communication: It refers to the exchange of ideas and information among personnel inside a company. It covers communication among staff members at various organizational levels, within departments, and with management.

Communication between a business and its external stakeholders, such as clients, partners, suppliers, and the general public, falls under this category. Customer service, marketing, public relations, and advertising are all examples of this style of communication.

Formal Communication: This kind of communication takes place in an organized, formal setting and usually adheres to a set of rules and guidelines. Meetings, presentations, and reports are a few examples of formal communication.

Informal Communication: It refers to exchanges that take place in a less official and more relaxed setting, often in the form of banter and dialogues. Informal communication may be equally as significant as formal communication since it promotes great workplace environments, teamwork, and connection building.

Verbal Communication: It refers to information that is shared orally, such as during face-to-face conversations, phone calls, and presentations. Since verbal communication provides for rapid feedback and the use of nonverbal clues, it is a crucial method of communication.

Written Communication: This refers to spoken and written communication, including emails, memoranda, reports, and proposals. Written communication is a crucial kind of communication since it leaves a lasting record of the exchange and is simple to access in the future.

Digital Communication: is the use of technology for communication, including social networking, instant messaging, and video conferencing. As businesses want to use the newest technologies to enhance communication processes, digital communication is becoming more and more crucial.

Importance of Business Communication in an organization

The following points demonstrate the importance of business communication in an organization:

1. **Aids in enhancing production:** By encouraging cooperation, effective corporate communication raises employee productivity. It fosters a relationship of trust and understanding between employers and workers. Understanding and collaborating with workers' needs and wants is a key component of effective communication. Employees are able to do their responsibilities more successfully and effectively by doing this. Additionally, good communication reduces the possibility of errors or mistakes being made while completing their task.

2. **Aids in growing the customer base:** Customers are an essential component of every organization, and good business communication may help in luring in new clients and keeping hold of existing ones. An organization's well-defined marketing plan and PR campaign work to attract consumers in its products or services and enhance the company's reputation with them.

3. **Strengthens company relationships:** Business communication strengthens business ties. It is crucial when interacting with customers or suppliers from the outside world of business. Vendors may need to routinely discuss their goods with customers to make changes. The future prosperity of a firm is also

determined by how well it gets along with other companies. A business unit may draw other business units for the purpose of establishing commercial ties with them if it has established its reputation as an entity for simple cooperation.

4. **Promotes company innovations:** Employees are better able to freely express their thoughts and proposals when there is effective corporate communication in place. Similar to this, good communication assures the efficiency of the sales team, market acceptance of the product, quick delivery of items in the market, etc. when any new product is introduced to the market.

5. **Information sharing:** An organization has to communicate with its internal and external stakeholders in order to share information. This aids in efficiently fulfilling its objectives.

6. **The creation of plans and policies:** Organizations may appropriately create their plans and policies via excellent business communication. These strategies and policies must be prepared using pertinent information. Through communication, many managers access dependable sources of information.

7. **Execution or implementation of plans and policies:** Managers are responsible for informing all levels of the organization about the developed plans and policies in

order to implement or execute them promptly. They may communicate strategies and policies to internal and external stakeholders by doing so effectively.

8. **Increase worker productivity:** Good corporate communication is essential to improving staff productivity. Employees are informed about various plans and policies, important problems, organizational objectives, etc. via communication, which improves their knowledge and helps them be successful at completing their jobs.

9. **Goals are attained easily:** Through good corporate communication, workers become attentive and

productive in their work, which leads to the prompt completion of their responsibilities.

VALUES OF EFFECTIVE BUSINESS COMMUNICATION IN AN ORGANIZATION

There are several Values to think about, but they all help generate outcomes. Here are some ways that successful communication encourages success:

1. *It fosters trust in one:* Leaders create a good example for their teams when they set the bar for communication across the organization. These illustrations promote cooperation, unity, and trust. When coworkers talk to one other honestly, the workplace becomes more trustworthy.

2. ***It fosters loyalty among the team members:***

   Team members feel appreciated and valued when corporate leaders engage in intelligent communication with them rather than just supervise them from a distance. Usually, this emotion leads to more loyalty and more work satisfaction.

3. ***Team member involvement is improved:*** While many businesses use innovative techniques to boost team member engagement, they often ignore the basics of honest, regular communication. A company is free to use whichever strategies they see appropriate. Nevertheless, without first ensuring that

leadership maintains an open channel of communication with team members, such techniques are likely to fail.

4. **_Teamwork is enhanced:_** The foundation of a cohesive team is excellent communication. To improve cooperation and peer connections, leadership should serve as an example of and actively encourage an environment in which communication is clear, direct, timely, and courteous.

5. **_It increases output:_** Team members that are actively involved and have a clear awareness of their tasks are often more productive than disengaged team members. Team members who

don't completely understand their responsibilities often become irritated or doubt their ability. If the information is easily accessible and presented well, team members may carry out their duties more successfully.

6. ***Communication stimulates creativity:*** Collaboration is encouraged via effective communication. Innovation thrives when team members are allowed to discuss ideas with other members and the leadership.

7. ***It finds solutions:*** Internal problems are often resolved (or completely avoided) by teams with effective communication that encourages attentive, active listening as well as courteous

and professional replies. The success of a team can only be enhanced by converting potential disagreements into fruitful and helpful discussions.

8. ***Better client connections result from it:*** When a business encourages effective communication among its workers, this positive habit often transfers to successful encounters with consumers. Effective and pleasant communication may be contagious. Customers value honest and open communication between the two sides, which only serves to increase customer confidence.

THE GUIDE'S OBJECTIVE

An organization's communication is its lifeblood. It serves as the means through which organizational duties are carried out effectively and objectives are met. The following Objectives pertain to corporate communication as a distinct subject of study:

1. **To create plans:** A plan is a roadmap for future activities. For the purpose of achieving organizational objectives, a plan must be created. Information is needed by management in order to create a plan. The goal of communication in this

situation is to provide the concerned management the information they need.

2. **To carry out the plan:** A strategy must be carried out after it has been created. Timely communication with the people involved is necessary for plan implementation. As a result, the goal of communication is to spread a strategy across the company for effective execution.

3. **To aid in the formation of policy:** Policies are instructions for carrying out organizational tasks. Policies are sometimes referred to offer permanent solutions to ongoing issues. To govern its operations, every company has to create a set of policies. Information from a variety of sources is also needed while creating policy. As a result,

the goal of communication is to gather data needed for policy development.

4. **Obtaining an organizational objective**: The combined efforts of managers and employees are crucial for accomplishing organizational objectives. The actions of workers at different levels are synchronized and coordinated via communication in order to accomplish the organization's stated objectives.

5. **To arrange resources:** An organization has access to many different types of resources, including human, material, financial, and so on. The managers' biggest problem is in effectively and efficiently arranging these resources. The solution to this problem is communication.

6. **To synchronize:** An essential managerial task is coordination. Large businesses' several functional departments are connected. Organizational objectives cannot be achieved without adequate and timely coordination. As a result, the purpose of communication is to coordinate the activities of many departments to make achieving organizational objectives easier.

7. **To give orders to subordinates:** A manager's responsibility is to coordinate the efforts of others. Management must guide, direct, and supervise the workers in order to complete the tasks. These management duties must be carried out with good subordinate communication.

CHAPTER 2

FACTORS AFFECTING BUSINESS COMMUNICATION

The sharing of information, opinions, desires, and attitudes between or among people is referred to as communication. Communication is the same in business. Business communication refers to the dissemination, retransmission, reception, and exchange of ideas in business and industry. When the receiver comprehends the message's meaning in accordance with how the sender encoded it, this exchange is successful. The meaning of a statement in business, however, may be distorted by a number of circumstances.

The meaning of business communication may be influenced by a number of circumstances, which includes:

Cultural Diversity

First Communication between persons with diverse cultural backgrounds increases the likelihood of miscommunication and incorrect message interpretation. A workforce that is culturally diversified is often seen in large firms and MNCs.

They also work with a variety of nationalities. A firm may find itself in a very difficult scenario as a result of misinterpretation of signals. Businesses may take certain actions to prevent this issue.

A Misinterpretation of the Message

When individuals interpret the same term differently, commercial communication also suffers. When technical terms or jargon are utilized, such a misunderstanding occurs. Additionally, individuals may purposefully misrepresent the true meaning of words.

Although message misunderstanding is typical in communication, it might be problematic for the business. Consequently, communications must be adequately planned, and a feedback mechanism is necessary.

Emotional Distinction

The meaning of communication is substantially influenced by the emotions and sentiments of the individuals involved. For instance, doctors often have a lower level of emotional attachment to their patients than do their patients' family.

Previous encounters

The efficacy of subsequent communication between the same sender and recipient is significantly influenced by the results of earlier communications. Further contact between the parties is probably not going to be successful if one of them had a negative experience.

Difference between Education and Intelligence

The meaning of communication is also influenced by the disparity between the informal educational and intellectual levels of the sender and recipient. Communication will be successful if their educational backgrounds are comparable. since it is possible that they share the same views, understandings, feelings, thoughts, and perspectives, etc.

Group Memberships

Differences in group membership also impact business communication. If the sender and the recipient are members of separate formal or unofficial organizations, communication. They can start to perform worse. For instance, the lack of contact between management and trade union officials may be the result of their animosity against one another. Similar to how official group affiliations based on gender, age, geography, or religion may influence corporate communication.

Positional Variations Among the Staff

The hierarchy of the sender and recipient may prevent effective communication if they are at different positions. We sometimes see individuals going too far in an effort to uphold the formality of the organization. For instance, leaders often give any communication from their subordinates less consideration. In order to minimize the labor and obligations, subordinates also strive to avoid following any instructions from superiors.

Sender and recipient functional relationships

The purpose of communication in business is substantially influenced by the functional connection between the sender and recipient. The recipient could not grasp the sender's message if they are from different functional departments or sectors. For instance, the message of the product design manager or the quality control manager may not be understood well by the finance management or vice versa. The expressing, rerouting, receiving, and exchanging of ideas in business and industry constitute business communication. The meaning of business communication may have an impact in a variety of ways. This impact may be favorable or unfavorable.

Organizations have difficulties when it comes to corporate communication. Different communication methods, cultural nuances, language limitations, and opposition to change are a few examples of these difficulties. Organizations may attempt to address these issues and enhance their communication procedures by being aware of them. When it comes to corporate communication, organizations encounter a variety of difficulties, including:

Communication Style Disparities: Because people communicate in various ways, this might result in misunderstandings and misinterpretations. In order to develop efficient cocommunication, it is crucial for firms to acknowledge and understand the various communication preferences of their workers.

Cultural differences may cause misconceptions and miscommunications because culture can have a significant impact on how individuals interact. Organizations must be conscious of cultural differences and make an effort to reduce barriers between workers from various cultural backgrounds.

Language Difficulties: Communicating in business may be quite difficult when there are language barriers. It may be challenging for coworkers to understand one another when they speak different native languages, which can result in misunderstandings and poor communication. To assist workers in overcoming these challenges, organizations need to provide language instruction and translation services.

Resistance to Change: Organizations often need to modify their communication methods to stay up with the fast-paced business climate of today. New communication methods may be challenging for corporations to adopt because certain workers may be resistant to change. By including workers in the change process and outlining the advantages of the changes, organizations may attempt to overcome these difficulties.

Technology has completely changed how businesses interact, but it has also presented a number of new problems. Miscommunications and misunderstandings may result from technical issues, cybersecurity risks, and the increasing usage of digital communication. Organizations must keep current with technology and take the initiative to solve these issues.

METHODS OF EFFECTIVE BUSINESS COMMUNICATION IN AN ORGANIZATION

Face-to-Face Business Communication

Face-to-face business communication is the most popular and effective kind of communication. Because it often takes the form of conferences or meetings, which is a face-to-face communication method. This calls for expert interpersonal abilities. This approach also incorporates body language and nonverbal communication. Body language, such as gestures and facial expressions, is very important when two or more people are conversing in business since it helps to convey a person's attitude toward others.

Better interpersonal communication may also be facilitated by having good listening abilities. The majority of corporate communication calls for active listening in order to comprehend quick exchanges.

Email as a method of communication

E-mail is now the most used method of communication in businesses. Email is regarded as one of the preferable techniques in corporate communication due to its ability to transmit and receive bulk or numerous communications at once. Additionally, because emails can be sent and answered quickly, efficiency is increased. Email conversations may include two individuals or more, and they are the greatest replacement for official face-to-face meetings since they allow for debate. email correspondence

Web Conferencing

Web conferencing is a type of corporate communication where communication takes place over the internet during meetings, conferences, presentations, seminars, and training sessions. It has capabilities like screen sharing, file sharing, live chat, recording, etc. This might be regarded as the most successful method of communicating with individuals seated in various places. Using the phone (teleconferencing) or video equipment, one may conduct web conferences (videoconferencing).

Additionally, teleconferencing is a popular choice for workplace business communication. When it is not practical for members of an organization or company to go to a physical meeting or conference, telephone conferencing is an efficient way to communicate. This also reduces travel costs since those who often travel widely for professional objectives may now conduct teleconferences while seated in their workplace. Similar to teleconferencing, videoconferencing allows participants to see the individuals they are speaking with. This calls for video conferencing hardware, which is organized by an organization's IT department.

Written Communication

This is more professional and thorough than other forms of communication in business. Formal letters, pamphlets, posters, and other written communication tools are examples. written business correspondence

Additional Techniques

Other corporate communication strategies include using an instant messaging platform. This technology is simple to use since it allows for quick connections with others while working remotely and quick dialogues.

Functions of Business Communication

1. Explaining work responsibilities to employees: One of the most important aspects of company communication is informing employees of their allocated job obligations. Team members may

contribute more to the completion of their assigned duties if they are clear about the required work responsibilities and how they can help the business achieve its goals by carrying out their job functions. Employees may be unable to execute their task as planned if their duties are not clearly defined.

2. Giving appropriate feedback: Another crucial role of corporate communication is giving prompt and correct feedback to both consumers and staff. Regularly giving workers feedback on their performance and capabilities at work helps improve their performance. This enables individuals to better grasp their skill set and capabilities as well as any gaps that may exist

due to a lack of necessary talents. The enhancement of the manufacturing process and quality is made easier with regular input from consumers and other stakeholders on the company's goods and services. An organization uses a variety of informational communication methods, such as job descriptions, performance management, and objectives that must be met.

3. Persuading clients: Business communication is often used to persuade current clients, potential clients, and business partners to complete a trade or transaction. A salesperson may persuade a customer over the phone or in writing, such as by distributing a mass advertising in a magazine or newspaper promoting the debut of a new product

or enticing deals on old ones. This communication function is heavily reliant on both credibility and emotions. Additionally, this kind of communication may be used in PR (public relations) efforts and to develop the brand image of the company.

4. Employee motivation for improved decision-making: Strategic communication is used in organizations to improve workers' capacity to make decisions about their daily tasks and long-term goals connected to the company. For example, if performance-based bonuses or incentives are successfully communicated among workers, it inspires individuals to contribute to the development of the business more effectively

and enables them to meet their job objectives on schedule.

5. Creating social ties: Communication is crucial in helping workers create a social network or link. Employers at all levels may openly speak with one another and their superiors in certain workplace cultures or environments. Other companies favor using a chain of command or hierarchy for communication. Employees perform better on the job when they have a social connection to the individuals they work with, such as their coworkers, superiors, customers, etc.

CHAPTER 3

DEVELOPING GOOD COMMUNICATION SKILLS AS AN ORGANIZATION

There are several approaches you may take to improving your communication abilities. Some of them include:

Give it some thought

There are several communication frameworks, but if you want to grow better at communicating, start by making it a habit to consider these 5 questions before you send any message:

- Why are you talking to me?

- Who is the participant, audience, or receiver?

- What are you trying to achieve?

- What actions do you want the receiver of the message to take as a consequence of it?

- What style will help you achieve your objectives the most?

You should take some extra time to consider how and why you're communicating if you have trouble responding to these five questions. Afterward, check your comprehension with your boss or other coworkers.

Be patient.

To ensure that your communication is truly accomplishing the task you need it to, prepare what you want to say and evaluate it. This particularly applies to written communications, therefore it implies to edit, edit, edit. Keep in mind that effective communication seldom comes naturally.

Make it simple

Almost usually, workplace communication serves a wider purpose. Everyone is busy. Make sure they don't have to struggle to grasp what you're saying or what you want them to do. When giving a presentation or writing anything, be sure to make your audience aware of your goal and key point right away. Then enter the information.

Condense

In ordinary business conversations, you don't want to be patronizing or "dumb it down," but you also don't want to make the other person struggle to comprehend you. Find a concise, unambiguous phrase to express your argument. To make your message obvious and remember, repeat it at the beginning, middle, and finish. You may also think about utilizing a straightforward illustration or metaphor.

Be adventurous and diverse.

Work on creating various strategies for various communication requirements. Try out one part of your communication at a time with your audience. Consider giving your informal communication structure more thought for a week. After that, experiment with various formats for official meetings or updates for a week.

Use and contemplate

Be intentional in analyzing your daily conversations to see what works and what doesn't. Maybe your manager's email wasn't received properly. Do you see how that may have been perceived incorrectly? What would you change if you could? Similar to this, consider if you adequately stated your needs if a talk with a coworker didn't provide the desired outcomes.

Keep the whole package in mind

To obtain insight into what your whole package communicates in your everyday contacts with your team, think about documenting a couple of these conversations. Do you gaze at people? Do you have a confident, comfortable, or strained facial expression?

Your body language is how? Do you provide time for queries and explanations?

Request input

A few dependable coworkers and your boss might be a good place to start. Start by asking them to evaluate both your written and verbal communication individually (i.e., on a scale of 1-10). then pose these 3 inquiries:

- What should I do first to improve my communication with you?
- What specific action should I cease taking in my correspondence with you?
- What one thing or talent should I focus on honing to enhance my communication at this company?

CHAPTER 4

USING EFFECTIVE COMMUNICATION TO BUILD STABLE WORK RELATIONSHIP

Why is good communication in the workplace crucial?

Because it increases employee morale, engagement, productivity, and happiness, communication in the workplace is crucial. For improved teamwork and cooperation, communication is also essential. Effective workplace communication ultimately contributes to improved performance for people, teams, and organizations.

To go even further, developing strong communication skills provides significant short- and long-term advantages for your business as a manager. A team led by an excellent communicator may do more with better outcomes and fewer misunderstandings. And who doesn't desire a reduction in miscommunications?

Types of Communication in a Workplace

Workplace communication is not created equal.

Everyone has had the feeling of sitting through a tedious, protracted meeting and thinking, "This should have been an email." Different methods of communication are suitable for various sorts of communication. Those many routes may either improve or hurt how information is received, depending on the kind of information being sent. A skilled communicator will hone various abilities and resources to correspond with the required sort of communication.

- **Leadership dialogue**

One-way communications are often given by leaders to their teams. The aim could be to update or inform, as in the case of a memo outlining a new business policy or a change in course. Leaders often use communication to convince, inspire, and build loyalty. More often than not, they convey information via tales.

- **Upward correspondence**

Managers (and team members) often have to interact with other leaders who are not directly under them as well as with their own managers. These might be memos or emails, reports, or a spot in a regular meeting. These messages, regardless of format, need to be regarded as more official.

- **Revisions**

Updates often fall short of being a sort of powerful communication since they are brief by nature. Save your vocal or written comments for calling attention to what is most essential, which is often what demands action or more engagement from the audience. Instead, rely on a visual tracker or dashboard to bear the burden. This may contain rewards as well as shocks, challenges, and possible hazards.

- **For good reason**

These formal communication activities often get the most attention. Presentations are communication tools with greater stakes that are often intended for a wider audience. They want to educate, influence, and persuade others. In addition, a lot of individuals are afraid of public speaking, and because of TED and other such programs, we have high expectations for both entertainment and knowledge.

- **Gatherings**

Large or small, meetings are an essential component of an organization's internal communication plan. One of the least understood and most misused forms of communication, they are also. Effective meetings foster team collaboration and swiftly convey information that may be easily misconstrued in another format (like email). The greatest meetings foster a lot of collaboration and leave attendees feeling energised rather than spent.

- **Communications with clients**

Customers may be communicated with in any of the ways mentioned above: one-offs, face-to-face, virtually, orally, in writing, or ad hoc. In general, all of the factors that affect employee communication also apply to consumers. Be careful and thoughtful when crafting your communications so that they meet the demands and preferences of your audience and foster a favorable perception of the brand and the item.

- **Informal exchanges**

Informal communications include the emails and conversations you have during the day to make requests, ask questions, get information, answer questions, and provide or receive help and direction. These informal conversations have the secondary goals of creating social bonds, fostering culture, developing trust, and discovering common ground in addition to advancing the organization's mission.

How to Improve the Effectiveness of Workplace Communications

Create a strategy for internet communication:
Businesses are very dynamic in today's digital environment, and technology is always evolving. It's likely that neither team members nor supervisors are aware of every communication channel that is accessible to them at any one moment. Then they could squander time at work looking into communication techniques that are already in use and available across the whole firm.

Businesses may want to consider creating and disseminating an internal communication strategy that gives team members a list of the current communication channels available as well as instructions on how to use them in order to prevent this unnecessary time drain.

This method may be seen by businesses as the main source of information for project communication. Team members should be able to use this knowledge to respond to inquiries like the ones below:

- What does each channel serve to achieve?
- How can I get in touch with coworkers in other departments?
- When should we engage in face-to-face contact rather than using a communication tool?
- Who is in charge of this project?
- What is the project team's composition?

- What methods are used to disseminate crucial project information?

Using communication tools

With recent technological advancements, communication in the office has advanced dramatically, setting new expectations for working relationships. These developments have produced fresh techniques for enhancing communication. Here are three instances:

Tools for video conferences: Team members may communicate remotely and discuss prospective projects, daily chores, and pertinent updates using video conferencing capabilities. These platforms also provide a way to interact with clients (and prospective clients) who are geographically separated. Tools for video conferences are relatively simple to use. By arranging a time for the meeting and providing participants with an internet connection, the meeting facilitator may arrange a video conference.

Internal conversation or messaging: Applications for private and group messaging are often more effective than emails and may be ideal corporate communication tools to keep teams together. Instant messaging and chats provide live engagement, simulating actual, in-person talks.

Venues for discussion: A forum that promotes open and honest debate of any issue among peers, managers, and leaders. Knowledge sharing is necessary for workplace community and internal progress. New hires may benefit from assistance from seasoned staff in navigating a firm, which can help them come up to speed more quickly and with fewer blunders. The company as a whole becomes more unified thanks to a digital workspace where workers can discuss initiatives, ask questions, and handle problems at work.

artificial intelligence writing aids.

AI writing Assistant tools

The main objective of artificial intelligence (AI) business writing helpers, like Grammarly Business, is to support all team members in creating effective messages. Though not everyone is a skilled writer, most vocations need efficient communication. These employees can create understandable material quickly and clearly with the use of writing tools.

How to communicate better while working at a distance

Having effective communication skills is crucial for managers and leaders who operate remotely. By doing it correctly, you may increase team connection and trust while reducing some of the difficulties brought on by misunderstandings.

To enhance distant communication, keep the following in mind:

1. Specify objectives

At the beginning of a conversation, be clear about your expectations. Even better, rephrase your expectations by asking the other person to confirm their comprehension.

2. Take part in two-way flow

Employees may find it simpler to detach and check out when they work remotely. Give people a voice in communication with thought and imagination. Use polling and ranking tools to ask questions and get answers in the form of emojis, gifs, or one-word summaries.

3. Keep in mind the impact of face time

Without other indicators like voice tone and face expression, a lot in the flat area of text might be misconstrued. Don't rely only on text or chat while interacting. A well structured team Zoom call or in-person meeting may improve communication and understanding, allowing participants the opportunity to bring up any areas of misalignment.

4. Put quality first

When working remotely, people could feel more guarded of their time, so plan live events carefully. Send meeting goals, agendas, or background material in advance to assist participants be ready for fruitful discussions.

5. Create a relaxed setting

Effective day-to-day communication at work starts with assuming that people are doing the best they can and with fostering a culture of sharing. However, without possibilities for informal connection like happy hours or non-work Slack channels, they are difficult to create and sustain.

6. Be considerate

You don't have to spend a lot of time digging up on individuals and getting personal information. It's important to keep in mind that the individuals who will be reading your correspondence are actual people with genuine issues, diversions, hopes, and anxieties. Try imagining the other person before starting a video conference or sending an email.

CHAPTER 5

ESTABLISHING AND SUSTAINING BUSINESS RELATIONSHIP

Building successful, enduring business connections these days requires a significant commitment of time and effort. Although they are so crucial to success, few individuals appear willing to put in the effort. Be aware that long-lasting business connections do not naturally arise or grow without persistent, committed labor.

We should have a competent, hand-picked network of business contacts that we can lean on for guidance, support, and insight. We need to strike a balance between giving and taking. Giving or taking is not enough; we need both. Too many individuals avoid asking for assistance when they do, which may be devastating to small businesses. Finding excellent individuals and developing connections with them need selectivity, consistency, and involvement.

Here are some strategies for creating enduring business partnerships in the modern workplace.

BE SINCERE

It's not that difficult. Be yourself, and accept people for who they are. Even online, it's simple to adopt a fake identity, but when we start vetting individuals and businesses, that is not the best method to build a connection. Find businesses and individuals with whom you can easily communicate and with whom you have a natural connection as well as areas of shared interest. Relationships may progress more quickly when personality, beliefs, and point of view are connected authentically.

DETERMINE COMMON OBJECTIVES AND VALUES

In life, we look for others who share our interests, aspirations, and moral principles. Are they trustworthy, kind, savvy, and helpful? How are they with other people? This has to do with moral integrity. Do they respect us? Sadly, I've witnessed far too many individuals who first show themselves one way, only to betray others after they gain their confidence. Even if we may not always agree on everything, having similar ideals is essential.

ENCOURAGE MUTUAL RESPECT

Unless someone is introduced to you by a reliable link, I find this takes time. We establish our worth through time and via a variety of endeavors and experiences. Join a chamber of commerce, a professional organization, or an online forum, which are all excellent settings for building contacts. Watch individuals in action and use patience and discernment. Relationships can only develop if there is mutual respect between the parties.

DISPLAY A LITTLE VULNERABILITY

We must sometimes share and help one another through adversity, hardship, and change since we are just human. Being vulnerable contributes to our authenticity. One word of advice: avoid sharing this publicly and instead keep it to a small group of people. Use caution in this situation.

I'VE GOT YOUR BACK

As a method of demonstrating your dedication to them, let individuals know that you have their back. I've attended far too many gatherings when people just shouldn't be engaging in gossip and pointless talks. As difficult as it may be, I have chosen to speak personally to a few individuals and politely requested that they rethink those interactions and decide not to continue communicating with them.

CREATE MEANINGFUL CONNECTIONS TO HELP PEOPLE NETWORK WITH EACH OTHER

A recommendation is the ultimate compliment in business. We should link individuals for the right reasons, be considerate, and have the correct motivations. Not all recommendations are successful. Don't do all the effort; it takes two to make it happen and work.

BE MORE PRIVATE

Ask folks out for coffee if you truly want to get to know them and have one-on-one, more intimate conversations. Be open to learn more about each other's stories, families, and careers by exchanging experiences, ideas, and points of view.

MAKE A FUN ACTIVITY TOGETHER.

Work without pleasure makes us boring! Be open to spending time with friends doing activities that may not include work. Meeting up with friends and attending community activities are all enjoyable ways to observe people from various perspectives. Not to mention the chance encounters, laughter, and discussions that may result from it.

LET EXPECTATIONS GO

Never presume and always enter relationships with an open mind and reasonable expectations. People are just what we perceive them to be based on the experiences we have had with them. Accepting that people are not always as you want them to be was one of the finest bits of advise I have received from a customer. We are setting ourselves up for disappointment if we have preconceived notions about others.

PLAN A TIME FOR BRAINSTORMING

Set aside time specifically for team brainstorming, interaction, and business. It's best to schedule a regular time, a time limit, and an agenda for the tasks you wish to do within that period. Give the unexpected conversation some time.

PROVIDE A SERVICE BEFORE SEEKING ONE

Serving is the new selling, according to a trend brief published by Trendwatching.com in 2010. They gave a term to a trend shift in sales and marketing that we already knew about, and now it is accepted practice in business, social media, and content marketing.

By sharing our knowledge and skills with others in an effort to inform, assist, and inspire them, we lay the groundwork for long-lasting connections. We are assisting and assisting others when we blog, provide content, talk, do workshops, webinars, publish e-books, and attend events.

We are assisting and assisting others when we become more serious and involved on LinkedIn, Facebook, Twitter, and other social media platforms where the community meets and shares ideas. Like nothing else, giving and helping others fosters trust.

CONCLUSION

Organizational success depends on efficient corporate communication. It makes it possible for businesses to communicate, develop connections, and accomplish their goals. Encoding, transmission, decoding, feedback, and interpretation are all steps in the sending and receiving of messages in business communication. Both the sender and the receiver must put out effort in order for the message to be correctly sent and comprehended.

Language hurdles, cultural differences, and noise in the communication channel are just a few examples of the elements that might hinder communication. Organizations must be aware of these issues and take steps to address them. They should also be aware of how crucial efficient communication is for creating dependable working connections, raising productivity, and succeeding. Organizations may boost performance and realize their full potential by investing in efficient communication techniques and abilities. Organizations should routinely analyze and evaluate their communication processes and, if required, make changes. This may include conducting surveys, obtaining staff input, and putting communication training programs into action. Utilizing technology and digital tools may also assist firms in enhancing their communication strategies and expanding their target market.

Organizations must also consider the many corporate communication formats and choose the best one for the given circumstance. For delicate or difficult topics, for instance, face-to-face contact may be more suited, whereas regular or less sensitive interactions may be better served by email or instant messaging.

Organizations must devote the required time and money to effective corporate communication if they are to succeed. Organizations may establish a healthy and productive work environment, enhance relationships, and accomplish their objectives by continuously improving their communication techniques.